AF211888

T.M. PAISLEY

POSITIVE CHILD GUIDANCE

The Comprehensive Guide on Your Child's Mental and Development Stages, Get a Useful Guide on How to Understand the Mental and Developmental Stages of Your Child

Descrierea CIP a Bibliotecii Naționale a României
T.M. PAISLEY
POSITIVE CHILD GUIDANCE. The Comprehensive **Guide on Your Child's Mental and Development Stages, Get a Useful Guide on How to Understand the Mental and Developmental Stages of Your Child** / T.M. Paisley – Bucharest: Editura My Ebook, 2021
ISBN

T.M. PAISLEY

POSITIVE CHILD GUIDANCE

The Comprehensive Guide on Your Child's Mental and Development Stages, Get a Useful Guide on How to Understand the Mental and Developmental Stages of Your Child

My Ebook Publishing House
Bucharest, 2021

TABLE OF CONTENTS

INTRODUCTION

Ideally all parents should have an idea of what to expect at various development stages their child is going to experience. Armed with this knowledge, the parent will be better prepared to ensure this development is experiences with the least possible problems as possible. Get all the info you need here.

CHAPTER 1

DEVELOPMENT BASICS

Synopsis

Through the knowledge gained on child development, the parent will be able to help the child when things are not going as it should be or it will allow the parent to pull back if they are expecting too much from the child at any given stage.

The Basics

Information on the activities and achievements will usually be quite well documented for the parent to make easy reference should they need information.

There is also information on how to direct the child to ensure the proper development targets are reached successfully and effectively.

Most of the information available on the development basics of a child would be focused on the following aspects:

There would usually be an approximate timetable on the prenatal development that would be the ideal benchmark to measure against.

There would also be information on the normal stages of child development which would ideally be broken into stage of about 5 years each, starting from birth.

There is also information available on the general development sequence to be experienced from the toddler stage through to the preschool stage.

These stages would also cover information on various levels of the intellectual, language, social interaction, physical, and any other development that would be deemed important by the parent.

This is especially useful for the parent who is concerned about ensuring the child's growth rate is according to the norm and does not want to be pressured into forcing the child to grow in areas where there is no need for such pressure.

CHAPTER 2

EXPECTED MILESTONES
FOR YOUR CHILDS AGE

Synopsis

The development milestone guide is a chart or a format that ideally depicts the child's skills within a very specific time line. These specifics are usually calculated based on the average growth rate mentally and physically by census taken from similar age groups around the globe.

The Norm

However the parent should also be aware that these guidelines on the expected milestones are just that, guide lines, and there is really no need to panic should the child in question be a little late in a particular area of development.

It is possible that some children will develop at their own pace thus there is no real need for the parent to be over anxious over the matter. However if the development is significantly later than expected, a doctor's advice should be sought.

The following is a very general guide of the expected milestone of what the child's development should be:

A few months after birth, the newborn will be expected to be able to respond to physical and visual stimulation. The bond with the prime caregiver will be established and evident in small ways such as a smile or the clutching with its fingers.

The baby will also usually be able to cry according to its needs and will respond to any high pitch sound easily.

Following this period of growth the now 4 month old baby will be able to grasp at object and squeal with pleasure while also being able to react to familiar voices and routines.

There will also be evidence of the baby taking a keener interest in its surroundings and sounds.

At 6 months most babies will be able to lift their head and move shoulders. They will also be able to better decipher things and its required responses. Some will even be able to make one syllable sounds.

These expected milestone lists usually go on till the teenage stage.

CHAPTER 3

GROSS MOTOR SKILLS

Synopsis

Gross motor skill usually involve the large muscles of the body which enables functions such as walking, kicking, sitting upright, lifting and many other necessary motor skill that would be needed throughout the various phases of a child's development.

The Larger Muscles

The gross motor skills of a child would very much depend on the muscle tone and strength where any sign of low muscle tone would be characterized as a severe possibility of the presence of a disabling condition such as Down syndrome, genetic or muscular disorder or central nervous system disorders.

The gross motor skills are very pivotal to the movement of major body parts and coordination between body movements.

Most parents are usually on high alert for the first signs of the weakness in this area and once identified will usually seek some form of re course to correct the situation.

The need to correct the situation stem from the parents concern about the weakness of the gross motor skill that can and will eventually effect the child's education and general progress as a normal developing child.

These treatments can come in the form of a team being commissioned to evaluate the physical or mental capabilities of the child and then getting a therapist to work with the child to address the specific areas of lack.

The frequency of the therapy needed would very much depend on the stage of lack in the gross motor skills platform.

There is usually an orderly sequence in which the skill to control the extremities of the body such as the legs, arms, hands and feet are all coordinated to engage in the desired activity in an optimal manner.

Although rapid development in this area is a good indicator of the progress rate anticipated, delays should not been seen alarming, as later development is not really unusual.

CHAPTER 4

FINE MOTOR SKILLS

Synopsis

Fine motor skill will usually involve all the smaller muscles of the body that work together to enable the child to execute certain functions such as writing, grasping small objects and fastening small objects without too much of a fuss.

Smaller Muscles

These skills are of course a very important part of the child development and any weaknesses detected will usually be seen through the inability of the child's capability to eat by themselves, write legibly or to perform other simple tasks such as page turning and personal grooming tasks.

Here too there should not be too much concern if the child does not develop such skill as other in the same age group would have already been able to do so.

There would only be a need to consult a medical professional if the progress to this level takes an unusually longer time frame than the norm.

However understanding that there may be some delays, will help the parent avoid becoming too anxious, which will also cause the child to feel this negativity which can be upsetting and frustrating for the child too.

The evident lack in this area would not necessarily be a devastating situation as proper intervention will usually be able to sort the problem out and thus help the child to work through these challenges and eventually be able to perform the fine motor skills even if they are not of the usually expected standards.

There are therapists who can assess the current abilities of the child and then design the corresponding therapy exercises that will help the child to gain some level of acceptable fine motor skills. Providing the child with toys and games that will positively contribute to the building of the fine motor skill would also be advised.

CHAPTER 5

COGNITIVE SKILLS

Synopsis

Cognitive skill would involve the activity of being able to process incoming information and break it down to what is being required and then make the necessary assessments and corresponding actions that will result in the needs of the incoming information.

Thinking

There are a number of levels involved in the cognitive skills and it is possible to train the body and mind in three separate categories which would be the sustained attention category, the selective attention category and the divided attention category.

The sustained attention category would require the ability of the child to remain focused on the task at hand along with the corresponding time frame it takes to complete the said task.

Selective attention would be the ability to remain focused on the task while at the same time being aware of other information or distractions.

Lastly the divided attention level would be dictated to by the ability to remember information while preparing to engage in other matters, also known as multi tasking.

There is also the consideration given to the long term memory capability and this would entail the child's ability to recall information that has already been stored in the brain.

This particular input is very necessary as the information would be required periodically and should be divulged as accurately as first perceived.

Short term or otherwise called working memory is where there is an ability to apprehend and hold on to information in a more immediate circumstance yet will being able to simultaneously perform a mental note of the said information. Lack of this capacity will create the need for constant reference to material that ideally should be committed to memory easily and quickly.

There is also the area of logic and reasoning that will be developed within the cognitive skills of any child. Here the child will learn to draw conclusions based on the information furnished.

CHAPTER 6

SPEECH

Synopsis

Besides looking forward to the child taking his or her first baby steps, speech is the next thing on the list that parent urge their kids to start. Babies are encouraged to speak as early as possible and when this does not happen, some parents tend to go into panic mode. This of course is not helpful for the child and neither will be benefits the parent.

Talking

Therefore it would be very helpful if the parent is aware of what is considered normal and what is not when it comes to the child's ability to speak.

Periodic checks with the doctor should also incorporate the question about the child's speech capabilities as this will help to better determine the speech condition of the child without being overly anxious.

Around the age of about 10 to 12 months the parent should observe the child ability to try and verbally communicate through various cooing and babbling noises.

This would be considered quite normal and if this is not the case, medical opinions should be sought. For the age group of about 12 – 15 months, the child should ideally start to make basics sounds that use the p, b, m, d or n range.

There should also be attempts to imitate sounds in single syllable. As for the 18 – 24 months age group, the child now commonly referred to as a toddler should ideally have a vocabulary capacity of about 20 different words.

The toddler should also be able to identify objects easily.

Children between the ages of 2 – 3 years will not be able to be quiet and be a chatter box. They would be able to speak in short sentences and thus communicate fairly well. This of course is a wonderful time for the parent as they would take delight in showing off their child's speech capabilities.

CHAPTER 7

SOCIAL SKILLS

Synopsis

Being able to have good social skills is very important if an individual intends to be part of society in general, and this is no different when it comes to the social capabilities of a child. Children should ideally be taught at a very young age the importance of being able to interact with other in an amicable and friendly manner.

Interacting

Children who are able to interest with their peer and with adults in a socially acceptable way will definitely sing success in forming healthy relationships as they grow in different stages of the lives.

The parent contributions to the ideal style would be to interact with the child from a very early age in the same manner that would be desired for the child to eventually extend to others.

This will be a good way to encourage the child to observe and proactive the same socially acceptable behaviors that would smoothen and initiate strong positive relationships.

The parents' interaction with the child should be with a lot of love and respect that would allow the child to feel totally comfortable and thus be able to build good bonds.

Once this is observed the child will more than likely use the same methods in their own attempts to establish social bonds with their peers. From the early stages of a child which would be the preschool age, the social interactions made would be the first contacts with the other children who would be categorized as the outside world.

This would be the first attempts of the child trying to form bonds with other for the intention of creating some connections outside the actual family unit. Thus teaching the child by way of good examples on how to be friendly and cooperative will help the child eventually successfully make their own connections with other children.

CHAPTER 8

DEVELOPMENTAL DELAYS

Synopsis

All parents' desire for their children to grow up healthy and wholesome, but sometimes due to unforeseen circumstances such ideal growth may not be forthcoming as expected. This is usually identified through delayed growth in certain areas that will act as alarm bells for the parents.

The Factors

When there is evidence of developmental delays in the growth process of the child, step should be taken immediately to explore options that may help to reverse such negativity and instead put the child back on the right growth pattern.

However in doing so, parents should also be aware that it may not always be possible to rectify these delays which inadvertently effect the ideal growth of the child.

When this becomes evident, then the next course of action would be to learn to cope as best as possible both for the sake of the child and for the harmony of the entire family unit.

Some of the areas that are usually significantly observed for its delayed growth are language and speech, vision, movements constituting motor skills, social and emotional skills and thinking skills which would be recognized under the cognitive skills platform.

Sometimes there are delays in one of these areas and sometimes the delays are evident if a few and this could be due to a variety of different factors such as a genetic defect which could be in the form of

Down syndrome, fetal alcohol syndrome which is usually caused by the mother drinking alcohol during the pregnancy, fragile X syndrome, which is usually an inherited type of cognitive impairment or several other medical problems that might develop soon after birth.

CHAPTER 9

CHILDREN'S MENTAL HEALTH BASICS

Synopsis

The ideal good mental health condition would be where the child is able to think clearly in social settings and learn new skills to adapt to the surrounding needs of the time and to also be comfortable with developing his or her own self confidence, high self esteem and an emotionally healthy outlook in life.

The Basics

In the quest to understand and provide well for the child's optimal mental growth the parent should be able to provide elements such as unconditional love from the family members, teaching the child self confidence and high self esteem standards, spending as much time as possible with the child to encourage social interaction and growth so that the child will be

26

comfortable in knowing how to extend the same to other new additions whenever and wherever introduced.

By taking the time to interact more with the child through play and other means of interaction, the parent will also be able to encourage the child to learn how to accept guidance and encouragements from other sources such as from teachers and supportive caregivers.

It will also help the child to identify safe and secure surrounding in which to interact with others. With the appropriate guidance and discipline, the child will be able to make all the various choices needed for optimal mental health growth.

CHAPTER 10

NURTURING POSITIVITY AND CONFIDENCE

Synopsis

Self esteem if often connected to the thought process that this in an important ingredient in promoting the ideal growth of a child's positive and confident demean or and outlook. This will also be the contributing factor to the mental growth and corresponding social adaptability of the child.

Self Worth

One of the main contributions a parent can make to developing this in a child's growing process would be to ensure there is also of positive nurturing styles using love, care and respects as the basis of creating a confident and sociable child.

When a child is taught to look at themselves and learn to accept and like what they see staring back at them, then the road to learning confidence will be established.

Making the child understand how important it is to be able to accept themselves and only choose positive improvements to make should there be a need for changes should be part of the nurturing process provided for by the parent.

It is important to always take the time and trouble to reinforce the need to build a strong self confidence attitude in the child, and this can be done with a lot of positive comments and encouragements.

From even as early as the infancy stage, the little one will be able to perceive its self worth when the appropriate responses are given to its various different cries.

In receiving this attention whenever the baby cries out for it, the first steps to building confidence will be made although at this point the baby really does not realize the implications to its mental growth.

Children too will eventually catch on to this as they learn how to do things according to what is acceptable and thus enjoy the resulting positive nurturing and praise that will help to also build their confidence levels.

CHAPTER 11

RECOGNIZE CHANGED BEHAVIOR IN YOUR CHILD

Synopsis

Every parent should be concerned with any changes in behavior patterns a child may display as these could provide significant information to the parent on what is actually going on the in child's mind and thus his or her world.

What Is Different

There are several benefits in being able to identify these changes and this ability to read into the changes can sometimes be the only means a parent has available to assist in how to tackle a particular situation.

Most medical experts will attest to the fact that a child main display of a particular behavior is usually formed by linking many smaller behaviors together.

30

Helping the child cope with or enjoy a particular situation would help very much if the parent was able to correctly identify the behavioral pattern, thus enabling the parent to give the correct corresponding assistance to the child.

In trying to understand the child, the parent would have to keenly observe the various reactions and displays of emotions as this will almost always clearly indicate the child's thought process of needs thus contributing to an eventual more uniform set of behavioral habit that can be more easily read.

The child will also learn to use the parent as their main example by observing the parents' different reactions and behavioral pattern and in some cases choosing to imitate these with as much similarities as possible.

Therefore the parent would have to be very careful in how they display their own behavioral patterns as they should be constantly aware of the children's capabilities and understanding levels of copying such displays.

Through such observations the parent will be able to better cope with the different variants such as a strong will child, a child that needs to be competitive always, a child that needs a lot of encouragement and provide the corresponding lessons as needed.

CHAPTER 12

ABOUT BIRTH DEFECTS

Synopsis

All parents are concerned with the various aspects of the children and this usually beginning right from the time of conception, and usually never ends. Perhaps one of the first concerns would be about any possible birth defects that child may be born with and how to cope as best as possible should this be the case.

What Can Happen

Birth defects are usually defined as any prevailing abnormalities of structure, function or body metabolism that may or may not be obvious at the time of the birth.

For the more obvious abnormalities, the relevant supporting teams will be able to assist the parent in either learning how to cope with the birth defect or help the parent explore all options available if any, to rectify the defect as soon as it is permissible.

The structural or metabolic defects would be focused mainly on specific body parts that are either missing or deformed in some way which may be caused by some problem with the body chemistry that was unable for some reason to create a complete and perfect baby in the womb.

These defects usually include cases of spina bifida, cleft palate, clubfoot and congenital dislocated hip and many other possibilities.

The defects caused by the congenital infections can usually result in abnormalities when the mother experience and infection before or during the pregnancy stage.

These infections will cause the birth defects and could be in the form of rubella, cytomegalovirus, syphilis, toxoplasmosis, Venezuelan equine encephalic, parvovirus and chicken pox.

The pregnancy period is usually a stage where precautions should be taken to limit the chances of the mother having to cope with the onslaught of deceases that might have very damaging effects on the fetus.

Unfortunately this presence of deformity is not always due to some infection as even seemingly healthy parents, are sometimes presented with a child with apparent deformities.

CHAPTER 13

ABOUT BEHAVIOR DISORDERS

Synopsis

All kids at one time or another have some form of behavioral problems, it is mostly quite an acceptable norm that most parent are usually able to cope with. However when a particular behavior pattern becomes consistent and destructive, help should be sort in understanding and rectifying the situation so that all parties will be able to cope.

Behavior

The more common and not really threatening or overly damaging behavioral disorders would include over active kids getting into mischief, playing pranks, being occasionally rebellious and other milder behavior patterns.

However when these seemingly milder patterns take on a more serious and sinister display of negativity then it can no longer be thought of as normal but now should be looked upon as behavior disorders.

The more common warning signs of such negative and often destructive behavior would be harming or threatening themselves, pets or others, managing or destroying property, lying or stealing, not doing well academically and even skipping school, early smoking, drinking and drug use, early sexual activity, frequent tantrums and arguments and consistent hostility towards authority figures.

All the above displays would certainly signify a problem child and the parent would almost always feel at a lost on how to cope in such situations.

The confusion and anger felt of both sides should be dealt with suitably so that progress can be made to try and overcome this negativity and help the child accept the idea of help with the goal of getting back a calmer and better behavior that others can live with.

Recent research has been able to show that it is not always outside circumstance that contribute to the negative behavior patterns but can sometimes be due to some disorder in the brain.

Lack of certain chemicals or simply the imbalances of chemical in the brain can be one of the causes for the behavior being experienced thus the need to explore this possibility too.

CHAPTER 14

MENTAL HEALTH GAMES FOR CHILDREN

Synopsis

Working with children who have mental health problems can be quite challenging and adding to this would be the complication that most of these children would not be willing and open towards the help being given due to the mental condition. Therefore using games as a stimulating factor would be a good and encouraging tool to start with.

Some Tips

These games can easily be sourced and purchased online or at any game stores. Due to the variety available the parent would have to consider the child mental condition and what it would take to stimulate it the best way possible.

It is not always necessary to purchase these games as some can be handmade or invention just from some intuitive imagination to suit the needs at hand.

Board and card games are usually a good way to stimulate the mind. These boards' games are usually specifically designed to address the mental health problems the child may be facing such as depression, self esteem issues, attention deficit hyperactivity disorder and many more.

These board games can also be used from a therapeutic angle which would encourage the child to be involved without being pressured to face the actual mental health condition head on. It can also contribute to helping the child practice improving of the social skills that most mental health problematic children shy away from.

This will also eventually help to improve the self esteem issues the child may be going through. The parent can also use traditional games but with the added feature of getting the child to make one positive statement about themselves each turn they play.

Strategy games can also be particularly useful tools as they too help to build the self confidence of the child during the course of improving on problem solving skill and improving on working as team.

CHAPTER 15

MAKE SURE YOU TAKE CARE
OF YOURSELF AS WELL

Synopsis

Exercise in the form of walking, running, cycling or swimming is recommended. If you are above the age of fifty, running is not recommended as it will put a strain on your joints especially on the knees. Swimming is the best form of exercise for all age groups and you can do this any time of the day. Just half an hour of swimming is sufficient.

It Takes You Too

Our body requires a certain amount of rest a day. When you have a child with you, you will find that you are easily tired due to the tension of making sure the child is fed, the child is safe and the child is getting enough rest.

You will be up at all hours to care for the child. All these activities will put a toll on you and make you feel tired. Try and get enough rest whenever possible. Even half an hour of sleep will do you good.

Another factor to maintain a healthy mind and physique is proper nutrition.

You must ensure that you get all the nutrition in the form of vitamins, fibers, carbohydrates and protein in balanced meals and supplements.

These food and supplements will ensure that your body receives what it needs and this will in turn keep the mind healthy and sharp.

Printed by Libri Plureos GmbH in Hamburg, Germany

9 786069 838051